Tiny Light Certainties

Ten Months until Death...

The Poetical Works

Of

Thomasine Westall

Published 2010 by arima publishing
www.arimapublishing.com

ISBN 978 1 84549 434 6
© Andrew Fuller 2010

Printed and bound in the United Kingdom

Typeset in Century Gothic 11.5/14

Swirl is an imprint of arima publishing.

arima publishing
ASK House, Northgate Avenue
Bury St Edmunds, Suffolk IP32 6BB
t: (+44) 01284 700321
www.arimapublishing.com

Introduction

I used to write spuriously, by that I mean some days I would sit and record my thoughts and dreams for three or four hours, yet then at other times, weeks would pass before I felt the need to transcribe anything.

The last few years have been such a rush, moving away from home at fifteen years of age was always going to be a challenge; but I knew it was the right thing to do.

I have to thank all of my friends, both those I knew before I died and those I have made since, without any of you this work would not have been possible.

Special hugs to C and B (you know why), see you both again soon.

Oh and T, J and E take good care of yourselves.

Anyway, these are my thoughts, my faults and findings

I do not require your praise or ridicule

Not even acceptance

I am

Thomasine

Ten Months...

Blood Kisser
Comfortable Memory
Head Food
Late Summer in Bed
The Dark Place of Feelings
A Story...Part One

Six Months...

The Breakfast Table
The Shadows in Paradise
The Morning Ritual
A Sin, but Pleasure
Revenge of Past...Part One

Two Months...

Wound Dressing
Centre Piece
Under-shelf
I am a...toy
Strange Place to be
Pain
A Story...Part Four

One Week...

Wished
Buildings have feeling too
Dull in, Shiny out
Going
Softly
Queen
A Story...Part Six

Eight Months...

Soul Summer
Getting it Wrong Again
Being for the Life of Dreams
Dust
Activity
Pieces of You
A Story...Part Two

Four Months...

Multiface
Painting Face
Four Cardboard Walls
We two are Fools
Go Some
A Story...Part Three

One Month...

Written Taste
You made me Man of Evil
She fell and broke
Angst write
Distance Disinterest...?
Revenge of Past...Part Two
A Story...Part Five

One Day...

State of Mind
Days in the Maze
Gods

Ten Months until Death...

The penultimate year at school and so many positive thoughts and dreams; yet I just knew they would end up like the flies trapped in the spare room...swept as detritus off the window sill every month as they failed to escape and make their dreams of freedom a reality.

Blood Kisser

I want the warmth of your blood
a taste I crave,
the sustenance I need.
Locked into your cells
the passion dictates you.
But fear in your mind chokes your heart,
you have fallen before and lost some part.
I can see in your eyes,
you must be guarded.
Do you think I'm out to hurt you?
Will I take what I want and give nothing back?
Push me away or give me the sack.
I've opened my heart, my mind, life and veins,
drink my blood
take what you want.

Comfortable memory

Awoke this morning with a Mr Men kiss,
not a patch upon the dawn.
It takes years of smiles to see so far
and when the eyes fail the ears take over.
From a conversation with my former self,
circling around the shadows,
reaching out for a new guide to life.
Watch me fall like and eight-month child,
stepping firmly on my toes to keep me steady.
Brings back the image of a race in Falmouth,
tight-clad legs and a lusted thought so unknowing,
makes one smile now,
helping to see just a little further.

Head Food

Suckle on the feed of my enemy-friend,
wishful thinking destroys the truth.
So not dream tonight,
for it will not come true.
Just cast your thoughts aside doodling,
or maybe just dithering,
you know what you want,
behind the polished bold-headed trip.
I ask you to experience the truth of my dreams,
I laughed,
    out of character,
        out loud you could say;
            for some applause I might add.
I was confused,
Perhaps you're also,
time now to laugh again with friends,
you thought you might never find,
except in some drunken stupor.

Late summer in bed

Sneeze loudly banging my head upon the shelf,
it's a funny place to be.
Thousands of different ways to lie,
cannot remember the last time I felt this badly,
oh yes it was yesterday and again tomorrow of course.
Strain to hear the whispers below, shush!
Change position to gaze at the waxed ceiling,
a different pattern every time you look,
can you see yourself,
you over there,
what do you think?

Back to earth with a bump,
the stereo stopped some time back,
strange you should wake now; alcohol worn off?
Now you are alert with eyes adjusted to the dark,
red, green, blue dancing before my eyes,
roll over; bang your head upon the shelf,
it's a painful place to be.

The dark place of feelings

A fading memory
yet I'm in here with you
and a lost friend.
Secret meetings behind my eyes;
have I lost you?
To one side we go
to a place we should not be,
question fears asked,
answers I do not want to hear.
Are you taken?
Is it her?
Can you not answer me;
fallen in love?
A lost friend found again,
slouched in my home; go away.
Then you're back in vision,
unwrapping green and red material in cellophane.
If I kissed you,
could I change your mind?

The English landscape we lived in that summer

I wanted to dwell in a country landscape, I think you did too.   A cool breeze ruffling our hair as we cruised down hedge-lined country roads, green, the sun beating down on our faces through the sunroof of your car. There were no restrictions on time, or other people's boundaries to answer to.

To pause in the shade of a huge green oak, a traditional picnic spread on a blanket from the boot.   No one around, we could be the only people left alive in the world; I know that scares you. The air so still and warm, punctuated by the soft cheerful chirping's of some distant nightingales or something feathered courting in a willow.

Going now for a gentle stroll down by a stream, clean and fresh bubbling to itself on its merry way to an unseen distant sea. Hand in hand, talking in soft tones almost to be afraid to wake the flowers from the afternoon slumbers. Pausing to wonder at the glimpse of a deer drinking cautiously from the stream, she looks up but the peacefulness was strong on glimpsing us she continues to drink undisturbed.
Taking of shoes and socks we sit next to one another and dangle toes in the cool waters. The blue sky and head beating sun had that intoxicating effect of sweet, sweet alcohol, a desire to be loved growing all the time.

Spending the rest of the afternoon lying in each other's arms feeling safe in warm woodland surroundings; alone without feeling lonely.   Until as the sun started to fall behind a far, far distant brow we slowly return to your car, parked on the grassy verge of a woodland meadow. I kissed you, as you held the door open, you respond a fire alight in your eyes. To return to our home, we had planned for this time and enjoyed it to the full; at times. And then no matter what would happen in the rest of our lifetimes, or days together we could always walk in that landscape.

That private English landscape, protected from the ills of the world outside, the peace we felt and will always feel lies within ourselves, well me. To take wherever we go and walk in there whenever we want too.

Eight Months...

So the course of true love never runs straight, then again I know that it needn't for it to be real. I'll spare you the fickleness of thoughts that flood through every teenage mind; boy or girl, the scary thing is that actually we're more similar than we like to imagine. Anyway I wasn't foolish enough to think I would find things any harder or easier than others.

Soul Summer

We stopped for tea at the Spring Motel,
wild flowers drifting everywhere.
The drive had been pleasant,
your smile told a tale.

We held hands as we walked through the door,
through the perfumed air-barrier and into a war.
Words fly like bloodshot glances,
cutting remarks make no effect,
together shared respect.

The table was set in the corner.

Through courses we wade,
some service sought after,
a multi-course passion feast
with a taste that lingered,
our eyes never parted.

Waiters fade into silence,
lights dimmed around us
sleepless nights forgotten
living at that motel forever,
together.

Getting it wrong again

Alone another night,
I had been grateful to find an ally,
but perhaps I was wrong,
just another wistful fantasy.
If you read this would you understand;
just who are you?
Have I grasped the wrong end of the stick again?
Is this a lie in my hands?
Do you notice,
or care?
How much does a broken dream cost;
to be forgotten again,
or was I?
Does my low opinion let me down?
Have I jumped to the wrong conclusion,
once more?
Talk to me and tell me a tale,
I'm hunting the Dark Continent
and seeking out what I want.

I'll be careful,
I might find it.

Being for the Life of Dreams

The shopping centre was vast,
I was there in a small group with you.
Alleyway upon alleyway,
a thousand choices from which to make.
    Bizarre, bazaar so many shops,
    a glass-fronted showcase of which to browse.
    But it's so warm and I was never so bored.
    The manager came to talk,
    bored again, so I went for a walk,
    through shops of fine brass and downstairs.
    A much larger sight met my eyes,
    though that man was still with me,
    to three girls he talked, so I left.
    Across aisles of plain clothes,
what was I looking for he enquired?
    I closed my eyes and found myself moved,
    a club, a Cavern perhaps.
    Dark walls everywhere, so smoky,
    neon lights flashing above a distant bar,
    black-clad women everywhere,
so full, little room to move or think; so don't.
A pipe and a drug, another mindless
    experience,
    wandering taking in views.
Everyone talking, but I cannot understand,
    or speak.
    Yet I'm happy and no threat do I feel.
    Blown out of the dream,
    before standing locked
    outside in a square,
    enclosed orange walls
    and glass surrounding.
    Deaf ears still with me,

you're face to face.
            I have emerged from your eyes,
        as you talk I cannot tell, but I want to
                don't leave, stay,
                    make a difference.

Dust

In the centre of a forest dark and dank,
little light to guide the way.
Tightly trees ageless and worn,
the life of so many species dependant to survive,
on the sap of time itself.
Behind the trees sprites laugh during play,
you look but cannot quite see them.
The sun remains elusive,
no easy way out;
make some sacrifices,
help is available if you know how to ask.
The clothes you wear,
sodden and clinging,
no comforts this far from home.

Although you do not understand,
you walk, arm in arm with the future
and her partner fate.
Coming of at a tangent,
bouncing of the satellites,
I can see many reflections,
friendly faces.
You look in the trees,
but they are not visible just shadows,
a cause for distraction smile a welcome.
They rush forth to hold your hand,
a guide into the forest heart,
your home.

Away day stargazer searching for a fallen star,
then found it in her pocket,
wrapped in a cotton ball,
sparked blue in summer shine,

pulled it from within,
the silk pattern commode,
traces of deepest seawater,
dribbling down your leg
and in the dust of moonscapes lost,
gaze upon the footsteps of past travellers,
memories of sparking in the palm of your hand.

Activity

Your life as an anthem to a football fan,
through the good times and bad unrivalled support,
even in the reign of heroes fallen now.
Locked in the smallest room,
four tight walls and tiny light certainties,
a sense of familiarity,
a warmth in pain,
you have been here before surely?

Your life in the centre circle,
surrounded by empty terraces,
their hollow echoes and schoolboy cries,
not even the wind billowing in the nets.
No black-clad anti-heroes to boo this time,
no one gives a damn anymore,
eventually they saw the lack of importance.
Live weeds the only witness too...
another forgone defeat.

But this time no more chances,
no better luck next time,
no new season to look for,
no hall of fame for you.
Sorry?
For them you should be.

Pieces of You

I have seen two sides of the same person,
people chip away at you.
They take what they want
and give little back.
Always apologising and to justify what?
But I don't want you to take something for yourself,
whatever you want ask for,
forget those people who do not really care.
Laugh at them out loud, not just in secret,
they drive me mad too.
Why should I be bothered?
Why because I've seen you sad,
Let's fights them off together.
If you want, don't say anything,
because it's a laugh, all of them.

Across sand...

To dream of walking across a land of baking sand, we're dressed the part, khaki shorts and shirts. I thought the land was probably well below us because the accent of the people here was strange; this met with agreement. Though familiar it jerks and unsettles the stomach. The heat could be felt singeing collars announcing tales and although we carried no water I knew that we could always find some no matter when we needed it.

We walked along a mountain road the steepest edge of a canyon, the cliffs on one side the darkest of drops on the other, unimaginable and hard the paces steadied and slowed. Zigzagged so we could never see that far ahead; as is life. Each corner was approached with trepidation we did fear, a fear of what lied beyond our knowledge.
It was true we and we walked around one corner and the whirling of helicopter blades filled the air. The gunship looked straight at us; firing its machine guns at us so we ducked back around the corner, out of sight and safe, or so we thought. Eventually we found ourselves at a ranch in the desert where a man lies dead, a gunshot wound to the head; who did it...was it you?

Six Months...

The dark months arrive and they remain my favourite season of the year. As others slunk into melodramatic stupors at the loss of light, I flourished. Christmas that year was strange, it is hard to explain why as it really was not hugely different to any others previous...maybe inside I simply knew that every Christmas after would be very, very different.

The Breakfast table

Sitting around a breakfast table,
pushing sleepy spoons awash with warm milk.
Not really hungry,
not for food, anyway.
Looking into your eyes,
I could only see the night before.
A left breakfast, I got up and stood behind you,
putting my hands on your shoulders,
through the thin material I felt your bones.
Sharp, your head rolled in response,
forever in a day
and for the life you wish.
On a spoon-fed whim call my name,
circle the table with me.

The Shadows in Paradise

Find me a paradise where fallen promises live,
many reasons to stay and watch all day.
Once upon the welcoming sandy shore I stood,
crushing painful seashells underfoot,
the loss of so many unhappy thoughts,
I wished I realised that in the alphabet of life,
others have thoughts;
unhappy ones too.

> Driven to distraction by some comments
> in the breeze,
> something's never rest,
> I wish it were I.

Passed by some strangers shadows,
react to their presence with mirth,
why not they scorn your life.
I cried for a week until my eyes bled,
the product of an unsettled night.

> Hazard a guess as too the conclusions you reach,
> hardly said a word to anyone,
> let alone you,
> now where are we?

The Morning Ritual

Lost in the warmth of a morning cup of coffee,
tackled the tortoise for the shower this morning,
lost again, third time this week.

                          The radio playing its hatred,
                              aloofness from the D. J.,
                       must be in a better world of his.
Makes me want to perform a vasectomy on his throat,
                              smile inside, if only.

Took the usual route to work and play,
stuck behind a smoke producing emmett,
wide-mouthed and sleepy eyed,
seems they only come here to annoy me.
Give them a blast as we pass by, no hurry.

          Park in the usual places,
          walk in at the usual paces,
          witness the same old faces,
          got to be some better plans here.
          Cannot even claim it is good for a laugh,
          you just put up and shut up, hopefully not forever.

A sin, but pleasure

Cannot see the wind for all the times I've been here,
walked along this stretch of road every day of my life,
now my shoes all but worn out.
All of everything so it is,
do you know how to start it all off?
Have you even the time to listen to the answers?
Sat in this chair swapped in velvet,
on the table my small object of desire,
share it with me; please.

How do you know if it's all true or false and does it
        matter?
Of course not but I'll pay the penance forever,
people always confusing jealousy and envy,
they're all such fools,
yet they don't know it.
No matter how often you run up the flights of stairs,
you fall asleep,
then you're back at the bottom once more.

If you are really clever you might find the entrance to
        the elevator,
no guarantee it will take you to the top though.
Remember that or else it'll strike back,
crashing you to the floor.

Revenge of Past...Part One

Sometimes there are secrets
black and horrid in their deeds
taken from the blood of the pure and sure,
children hopping yet never knowing their fate.
From a familiar face presents flowers,
white hair and open smile
barmy madness as daggers fall
and blood flows,
as the old shall fall.
There are many columns in this world and walls,
to find the past and room,
so much rain.
The old they bicker and quibble over details
economies no longer adding to the promised
and still they plot.
Saw life as relief, or a mask, or relief
And the horror still continues.

That which is black and horrid rises again
yet many about are caught unawares.
I still see the young faces looking,
hopeful
and still the rain continues
and the horror is once again faced,
though all but one are unaware
open the door,
it slams shut,
and face to face with blackness.

There is a trial to mislead,
a pace to threaten the mad and black
before the truth comes out
and the demands will be after your soul.

Too a giggle and a swindled laugh,
the end has never been nearer.

                    Standing in rain
                    fear of everything
                    it is all coming
                    taking, destroying.

Four Months...

I swear I felt my biological clock ticking away; is that possible? Maybe it was just the threat of an early Easter; after all I'm only a teenager. Then again, if I died at twenty, would I know at the age I am now that my life is almost run? Even now I don't know the answer nor do my friends; I guess that means there is no right or wrong explanation.

Multiface

Face the facts Multiface you don't know what you
    want,
perhaps a regal ceremony implying your love,
but cast down from the blackness of youth forgotten,
swim against the tide make a point of life.
Choose the unexpected and make others justify
    themselves,
ask so many questions, that costs nothing.
When you know the answers,
time to make your choice.
Don't forget your friends, some past,
fallen under viscous lies,
never to love again.

Painting face

With a smile that could charm any soul,
or cut through confidence like butter,
        is it getting colder in here or just my imagination?
I thought it was all under control.
A kind of fine old oil painting left to long in the rain,
a puddle of multi-coloured essence dribbling away,
            lost forever wasted on a girl who will hurt you.
You go looking for the answers whilst wallowing in pain,
yes behind my masque I have changed at last,
turning from your shadow to your would-be companion.
No longer begging for your answers or explanation,
while you are not here I have planned,
the future from the past.
Kneel and face your master,
                    with your destiny at hand.
If you want to unravel these feelings,
a photo forgotten in the mind of a child-like adult,
it just doesn't seem important anymore.

Four Cardboard Walls

Spent some time at your house,
    never really felt comfortable,
        within the confines of smoky rooms,
            always feeling the weight of tales told.
              From the corner of your mothers eye,
                suspicion and searching questions,
                  wish my anger could be presented
                    so well.

We two are fools

Scream as loudly as you can,
you got it wrong again, admit it!
Have you ever wondered why you don't listen to
     yourself?

                                                    Fool.

And once again next time,
have you learnt your lesson?
Use that plan you had,
slowly yet surely; to seek out success.
Every time in the past minor wins,
followed with massive failure.

                                                    Fool.

No one will guarantee a win or a loss,
the chances decrease week upon week,
if you're lucky,
cover your options widely; you know it's right,
it worked before
and will again, slowly the seasons so long.

                                                    Fool.

If you were not you wouldn't write this,
will you ever learn?
Or maybe you should cut your losses now,
before they become too large for you to bare.

Go some

Turn to me and look me in the eye,
the words come, but you are frightened half to speak.
Say goodbye,

some surprise was etched upon my face.

I paused for breath.
The words are on my lips,

I am sorry…
but I didn't even know you had arrived.

And south

Grass so high moist against my skin as I ran through it. In
the deep south where I lived the sun was so hot, even at
this early hour it was almost unbearable. The grass gave
way to sand and I leapt from the riverbank into the cool
waters, the waters so calm and I swam easily to the
other side. I grabbed hold of the jetty and hauled
myself onto the creaking wooden pier which strode out
confidently into the river.

I sat dangling my feet into the water whilst the cat
watched a little bored, wagging his tail slightly, far to hot
really not to be in the shade. From down the jetty soft
footsteps, I turned to see my friend bringing cool drinks;
she sat next to me causing the cat to vanish into the
bushes scattered around the end of the jetty.

Two Months…

Okay, I told myself, 'you had known all along things were wrong'. Situations had become forced, contrived and I had begun thinking of others…but I hadn't met them yet. Fortunately some friends will always loyal but even over the next few months they couldn't stop me falling.

Wound Dressing

I found myself wanting something from you,
perhaps a light to guide my way; so unfortunate.
Do you realise what you have?
Understand me, as we walked arm and arm,
me in your shadow, cowering from sunlight.
I follow, sparkling figurehead you are,
rain crushing those newly flowered shafts of life,
my hands bleeding,
staunch them.

Do I love you in vain?
A pain pleaded to be blocked;
my past revealed.
So scratched over with no interest,
not what I was,
will you be my keeper?
Needing no others,
nothing would bring us down
flying high
are you're mine.
At last.

Centrepiece

Paint the structure with some patented gloss,
change the appearance to be deceptively pleasing,
but check what lies beyond that lacquered finish,
reflecting light to please you.

Fix it in place and admire for a while,
cast aside the doubts of others held before the viewing.
If you pace back and forth hiding the flaws,
from your minds eye it becomes what you desire.

In your eyes tonight you will see the fire,
set between posts of wood as you requested;
now admire.

Undershelf

Found the words I had written on the underside of the
shelf,
buried above a pile of books.
I remember the night I put it there,
we won; a good vibe,
staying up on my birthday,
you wouldn't understand.
Looking at the shape of the letters
and their basis.
I can see what I was aiming for.
Reading this you can start to see the results,
I guess you will still not understand.
It is one of those things you just cannot
explain,
not without seeming a fool
and I do that too well all ready.
I still play the same music as well,
although sometimes only in my mind,
memories of so many nights,
alone in my room on the bed,
or in it making no difference,
fills me with hope for the future.
Crazy is it not; if I explained it you might see it too,
but I cannot take the risk.
So from you the words will remain hidden,
the music is there in front of your ears,
whether you ask for it;
I laugh to myself.
You have heard it already,
but blindly you do not know it,
I find that amusing; not funny.
Even at this stage of life I see it,
what I wanted then,

did I know you?
Yes,
that was all very well,
the words style cuts back in,
it says go on; so I do,
but I did not know you then,

is it still relevant?

I am a...toy

If I curl my lips around you,
would you make me your toy?
A plaything for an hour or two,
be careful, I will outshine you,
become my prey; why not?

Although I am probably not that sort,
so carry on fading away,
until as a ghost you haunt my past
and I will try not to laugh at your memory,
to others I am the same.

Then maybe one day we will meet again,
two different people once where friends,
reflect upon what was once,
I am a soul of discretion.

Yet you will know something is wrong,
when you start looking for solace,
in the toys of youth.
Familiarity breeds warmth,
a contentious fear of safety,
but the position has yet to change.

Surroundings masked in shadows
and if you purchase enough,
can you make the past come back?
I don't think so.

Throughout the year fluctuating moods,
resulting in spasms of zest,
until finally you forget your purpose,
spending your life in a
Decepticon summer.

Strange place to be

Knowing peace in a place like this,
is so very, very strange.
I guess when you get down to it,
the peace is inside yourself,
not where you are.
Everything is restricted by something.
Time to go out,
time to come home,
another question breaks our discussion.
Leave us a lone for a while,
let us talk in peace,
in a place like this,
so very, very strange.

Pain

How many times have I said this in different ways?
Too many times that's for sure,
don't sneeze so!
Time to forget all you want; start afresh,
forget the past plan to the future,
someone else's stories,
or so they say,
who are they?
Finding the gap in your defences,
I know that one hurt.
Pleased to say I'm so sorry,
if it makes you feel better; I cannot tell.
Play for sorrow one last time, but this not it,
it will begin again I just hope it is so.

So cold up there

Have you ever wanted to visit the Arctic? I cannot say I have, but there I was standing in a line of twelve waiting my turn to disembark from the plane. It was not what I had expected, it was all huge grassy mountains; it seemed more like the Welsh valleys. Never mind the weather closed in all to fast.

Then locked in several small cabins sheltering from the grey blizzards that battered the extremities of our new world; but the time soon came when our presence was not wanted and we had to leave, a long walk home some might say and of course I was the last to be ready. I was almost left behind.

Then walk home began. We knew the bad weather was coming, two maybe three days to get home before...we were not told but we had to get away. So we walked, so very far though; Bournemouth Gardens no less and though we were so very close to home we could not stop, we had to carry on to find our reasons for travelling.

We're still travelling at this moment.

One Month...

Summer comes and brings so many forms of joy; wonder when I'd start smiling...funny enough sooner than I thought.

Written Taste

Put yourself in my shoes for a moment, I ask
see yourself through my eyes,
maybe then you see me.
What makes me tick, what makes me sick?
You will see the way I regard you,
the passions that dwell deep inside.
It's not easy when you feel so incapable
of being loved by one so loveable.

To many questions,
so many reasons never likely to meet us,
and yet a plateau of peace waits.
But the silence is painful,
the not knowing stabs at my heart.
Jumping to the wrong conclusion,
as usually an easy solution to make.
Questions best left unanswered,
but there is no such thing,
so talk to me now,
say the words I want to hear, for the reasons you know.

Tell me that we travel together,
say you want to be with me.
So when you look at me
think of the way I see you
and tell me what you want.

Intrigued by words on card,
a half-cast promise taps at my window,
shall I open it and let it in?
I believed the words that you wrote,
it was just what I wanted to hear.
Did you mean them?

Positive feelings all around,
lost in a week of last sorrow.
My mistake, did I get it wrong again?

I'll know in about half an hour.

You made me, man of evil

Don't talk to me about silence,
don't talk to me about being sore,
      I watched you cut your wrists,
      then not talk to me anymore.
            You asked me for my ears,
            asked me for my soul,
            but when I pulled my heart
                      out,
            not talk to me at all.
      You crammed me in your cupboard,
      when your friends came round to play,
      then woke me in the morning,
      said I couldn't stay.
You change your mask to suit your mood,
down to the last drop of blood,
running up a spiral staircase;
emotions come in floods.

        You stopped talking some months ago,
           left me and my thoughts,
         now look at what you made me,
           the creature that I sought.

She fell and broke

A studious woman awash with desire,
fallen through sorcery for burning heartache.
Having embarked upon a path to glory,
embitter with lucky friends,
swoon higher.
These feelings she harbours she cannot understand,
why blanked back by stony gazes.
All her friends now swallowed in velvet hush,
across a room violent emotions out of hand.
With targets set she fires a broadside,
occurring less each day what they think,
or say five minutes,
to forget after ten more.

This voice in your head says 'you're better of dead',
as your friends run away from your shadow.
When people call your name they say you're the same,
planning your fall from power.
Can't control your feelings so people send you reeling,
fade to the future your pride in tatters.

No more is she willing to hide.
What surprises more is sudden lack of sense,
she used to realise others mistakes and sympathise,
now she seeks another to wallow in depth with,
until a voice clears,
shallow mists are tense.
Now reflect upon a bursting loss of belief,
is everything you thought mattered wrong?
Do you heed the feelings,
reflect upon the meaning;
or sleep in tarnished grief?

Angst Write

Faced with a blank page,
searching for words,
always feared I would end up writing this letter,
always hoped I never would.
So help me if you can,
you're the source of my writing distraction,
a normally quick,
intelligent mind;
is blocked with the writer's pain.
I do not want to hurt you babe,
or make you tired and angry,
I just want you to know,
that I have always felt this way.
Let my passing be a joyful time,
now that the future is clear for your plans,
just spare me a thought on my birthday.
I have filled the page with memories,
I ask you to search your thoughts,
it has always been ironic.
My feelings I now hide,
Until we see eye to eye.

Distance Disinterest...?

On a Hammond organ kind of night,
drink to the whisky that pampers your moods.
Velvet lined dreams washed down to the depths,
of my thoughts.
Rising, mimicking the submarine,
Every Saturday, thinking of you,
more so in the week.
Today again I have seen you,
watched closer than before.
All often charm,
spontaneous smiles and distant disinterest,
so unsure as to speak and say.
Despite the support of others my 'friends',
do not know what to say at work,
maybe should try the obvious approach.

A curved shape,
a form or vowel,
so you think you can hide within?
Watching the same scenes,
over and over and over,
sorry still so cool!
You know like when you await for the inevitable?
Am disappearing in a black water sigh,
Downstairs,
a black clad swish,
as you see my tale
and come rushing after me,
if only you were free.

Revenge of Past...Part two

And darkened plots continued
smashing and breaking through views
two souls are preparing to make a stand.

There was age and refinery in their manner
they came from times past
memories clinging to their souls like foulness to a corpse
and there was fear on the mind of everyone.
The rain fails to rinse away the stench,
making the dark soul easier to find
she waits and knows what is about.

Retching takes about her,
she encompasses those about her,
dragging some under, flattering others,
softening the blow as they stand at her gate
whilst still the rain falls.

Through the muddy veil souls rise
pulling down walls, opening senses to their presence.
There is no more laughter
as two souls confront their nemesis
and god himself would weep.
Secrets fell,
cedar to flesh.

Retribution wears sparkling blue and red
unforgiving faces from the past
yes they know the fate awaited.
Their words shall appear teasing
Machiavellian even in substance
it is fear holding back perception of truth.

Two souls leave together
a bloody trail their wake
the past catches up with its deeds
evil begets revenge.
Not even the tears of gods shall save,
the blackest of souls this time.

Four friends and I spent the day in the open

Sat in a field, cornflower blue and peaceful; see the trail we made from the road and the circle in which we are. I have four friends with me; Ligea, Parthenope, Leucosia and Suspiria are their names. They are not human, of course, although they are of this world, sprites; my companions in life. Ligea is tall with wild red eyes, amber hair and a slight body swathed in blood red velvet so fiery and beautiful. Parthenope is also tall with sparkling blue eyes and blonde hair flecked at the tips in blue. She is dressed in velvet and silks, midnight blue, cool and calm. Then there is Leucosia my earthly spirit. She is slightly smaller and dressed in green; her joyful sparkling green eyes link my soul to the earth. Finally there is Suspiria. Swamped in black velvet, her tall pale frame perfectly appointed with black hair and piercing dark eyes remind me of my vulnerabilities and their solutions.

Despite their names they are neither Sirens nor killers, maybe so. We are upon the floor in a group playing with the flowers and talking. They bicker expertly but never fall out. Ligea and Parthenope are the worst, flip sides of the same coin. Leucosia is always joyful, she sees beauty in everything. Whilst Suspiria remains mostly silent, what she says is often brief and to the point.

To spend a day here is too little, but helps for now. Whenever I need them I call on them and they are there. We will join them again.

One Week...

I found my peace...brief though it was. The end was coming; the school year of course...not long to go; then again, I wouldn't make it.

Wished

Who says you cannot have what you want from life?
I plan to live forever,
or die trying.
I know what I want
and where I'm going to be,
or I think so anyway.
We must dream sometime,
but I do not think anyone has invented,
a super glue to fix broken ones, yet.
Maybe I could invent one,
I would probably make a fortune,
mainly from myself,
or people who met you.
Woeful self-pity
get a life.

Buildings have feelings too

Showers cascade onto an opaque structure,
standing abstractly,
softened by indifferent surroundings.
People do not care for the thoughts of monsters,
they simply pass by reflecting briefly upon a cure.

Perhaps the removal from sight,
a barrier or destruction,
such a shame the loss of someone's pride and joy.
Flushed once with success but becoming an anomaly,
at the end of the run no more production.

Now floundering abandoned despite desperate
attempts for attention.
If only some foresight could be found to save the
structure,
battered by winds and rain and careless souls,
create and destroy,
then gloat on what is done.

Some time passes and the skyline is cured,
the only memory on a photograph half
forgotten,
tucked away in the folds of a newspaper.
A memory someone might hold dear,
later in the century it could be missed,
but not by many who mattered.

Dull in, Shiny out

I travelled far on a shiny day,
looking for myself in another's eyes,
could not pause for thoughts,
just play,
take a chance from now despite the lies.
Hold onto the dream inside,
cannot plan for a rainy day,
everyday it rains inside,
hurts so much I have to hide.
Picking up some treasure left upon the shelf,
been there for ages out of sight and mind,
put it in a bag,
so much wealth,
I will share it out,
that is too kind.
Put upon my heart scars you see,
in place via a fury,
all change about the scene.
A pool of multi-coloured light and sound,
that is your life,
now gone,
did you enjoy it?

Drinking your cup of sorrow,
try not to drown once more,
pass it amongst your friends to sup
and wallow again.
Then everyday and in every way,
the thoughts come back to haunt you,
your anticipation does you credit,
it is a shame in a way,
but it is start.
I suppose I must not complain loudly,

or lose my direction and with it,
my will to succeed,
as you have.
So admit it for once in your tiny life,
you were wrong.

Going

I forgot you.
That says everything I mean to you.
No sparkle in your eye,
gone as you smoke.
Scratching for straws to float myself,
because I'm falling, rapidly.
Life in decline, all over;
now.

Softly

Dream dressed in velvet,
I wished I was.
Crushed within the confines of a vessel.
now I have escaped,
not silent anymore.
From the beginning so unsure,
could I make it all right?
Then a friend said take a chance,
to be invited to a dance would be,
like a dream, dressed in velvet,
I was.

Queen

She sat in midnight blue,
set deep within confines of stone.
Taken to her home,
but I did not know her yet.
In there swallowed by time,
waiting for thoughts answers,
from hands of others come words,
a seconds' thoughts,
that was all it took.

She sat in ruby red,
set within confines of youth and friendship,
out on a limb,
              or a prayer.
Sometimes it came so easily,
your face reflects my words.
A fracas in my minds writing made you see light,
all your tears dried,
there had always been an answer to why?

She sits in emerald green,
controlling all about her,
her influence spreading,
                 radiating,
                     prevailing.

She sits as only the queen ever can.

Confined inside

I was vaguely aware of the struggle that had bought us to this pace of metal and plastic. It was dark; lights were strategically placed to force shadows about the tables and chairs we were strewn upon. There were questions to be answered, repeated questions that I knew the answers too but was refusing to answer. There was glass on two of the walls, two way mirrors I felt sure and though I knew that we were being watched, indeed even examined, I could not see another soul outside this room. Eventually we were left alone.

The other people in the room seemed to be sleeping but I took the opportunity to examine more closely the glass. I laid my hands upon the cool surface and looked closely at the surface and yes there it was a scar upon the surface.

I placed my eyes to the scar and found that I could see through to the other side and to the people that dwelt there. There was row upon row of desks, at least thirty, and each had a similarly dressed person seated facing the glass. They wore black and blue and headphones; their attention was not on me though they were all taking notes on something.

I remember putting pressure upon the glass and then standing on the other side before running for the stairs opposite; it was then that I felt the heat.

Reaching the top of the staircase I found myself sailing majestically down a narrow river. The scenery, heat and attire of the locals led me to believe that I was in India. I mingled with the other people on the deck, no one seemingly paying me any attention; in return I paid them none. The journey lasted approximately an hour, I felt no fear of capture until we neared the station at the end; the place of our arrival.

I wormed my way through and then down the dusty winding road towards the town. The shop was plastic and neon filled and just about as complete a contrast to the outside world as one could possibly imagine. Was I naked? For people looked at me constantly watching and wary, the shop assistants whisper and gesture as I made my way about the tall stacks of books and magazines. The whispers touched my ears and told me it was so the fear was high. I remember leaving and walking back to the station. I do not know why I went there or what I hoped to find, but the fear remained the same as before I was in the station and lost again.

One Day...

I remember feeling...it's hard to describe, but I call it 'possible'. It was as if every moment of the last fifteen years had been leading me to this point. I had the answers...the questions are about to be asked.

State of Mind

Last night we travelled miles together,
a group that journeyed forever,
across hills of orange stone, gliding smoothly,
over and over.
An amber sky flecked in blue, sparking reflections,
onto regular lined cars, stationary,
those parked becoming burnt and rusty.
Nearer and nearer,
I saw creation turn to decay.
A gap appears and we stop,
our carriage turns from four into two,
easy enough to move, safe.

Through the stone door and change.

Rich and decadent,
blood red colours surge across the floor,
For tickets to Portugal on sale at the desk.

Do I know her?
That women,
recognition, but blanked questions.
Handed a bitter memory
but ask no questions now,
later,
no names,
not needed.

You and I went to dinner, my beautiful Lady
too a private affair
for the rich and famous.
Dressed to impress,
you are perfection,

hands held you and I move inwards.
I've led you away,
you wanted to stay
why?
I don't know,
but you came back
and the journey continued again.

Days in the Maze

Cannot see where I am going,
running around the maze of
concrete blocks,
should I embrace them?

Yes uncertainty is the only sure thing,
behind every corner a different question lies,
in the end even debating left from right,
feel the doubtful edginess of a child.
Like learning to ride a bike.

Untarnished by years of wandering,
crying to yourself in the shadows,
makes you feel alright when you shrug your shoulders,
so long as no one sees you that is.

The walks of the maze identical,
leading only to a false sense of security,
but the paths still impossible to negotiate,
if you find your way through,
more by luck than judgement,
maybe that the key to things
and at the end when you scream for solace;
you realise you are alone.

Back at the beginning,
once more you find yourself in knots,
many give up; few succeed to the end,
not without scars, whether they show or
not.

Turn and turn falling away,
sleepy towns snore so loud.
Woken by bright lights,
a lure to the big town.

Fighting to make the dream come true,
squabble with your namesake,
before closeness forces you away,
perhaps too similar to choose from.
And on another day do you find it?

What you where searching for I mean.
I was crying out for the answers,
I already knew them of course,
but I am a fool to see it,
maybe tomorrow.

Gods

We lay amongst the bones of a long fallen church,
Pillars for ribs smashed, as if only from the strength of a
god.
We were five, together and alone
Joined by more than the need for love.
To my north lay blood red,
Sensuous, rich and fiery
I need her passion.
To my east lay emerald green,
Earthly, mortal and stable
I need her neutrality.
To my south lay midnight blue,
Ambient, soft and moody
I need her life.
To my west lay raven black,
Dark, mysterious and unforgiving
She is my death.

Who am I?